# Against Music

[Poems]

Raphael Maurice

Kansas City     Missouri

Spartan Press
Kansas City, MO
spartanpress,com

Copyright (c) Raphael Maurice, 2021
First Edition 1 3 5 7 9 10 8 6 4 2
ISBN: 978-1-952411-49-6
LCCN: 2021931296

Cover image: Mike Keth
Title page image: Jim McGowin
Author photo: Christina Maurice
All rights reserved. No part of this publication may be reproduced or transmitted in any form or by any means, electronic or mechanical, including photocopying, recording or by info retrieval system, without prior written permission from the author.

Acknowledgments:

I would like to thank Christina Ann Maurice without whom this would be nothing. I would also like to express gratitude to Jeremiah Driver, all of my family who guide me with grace, and a special dedication to Mark Davidov whose insights and ideas are unmatched. He is a force from whom I steal always.

Some of this work has appeared in *Barren Magazine, Vending Machine Press, Word for Word, Ghost City Press* and other publications.

## TABLE OF CONTENTS

[Trailer Trash] / 1

[The Ticket to Heaven] / 2

[A Victory] / 4

[A Small Bestiary Within] / 12

[Adventures in Dentistry] / 14

[Mother's Day Sonnet] / 15

[As it is, I] / 16

[Goodwill] / 18

[American Standard] / 19

[Tonight] / 21

[Sympathy] / 23

[Champagne] / 25

[Christina] / 27

[To Be of Use] / 28

[Here Again] / 29

[How We Grew Thirsty] / 30

[Simple Song] / 31

[Sneer] / 32

[We're All Hunting Something] / 34

[The Piano] / 36

To Our Future Child

*Without music, life would be an error.*

-Nietzsche

# [Trailer Trash]

*And I'm sorry if I dissed you.*
       -Modest Mouse

A German called out more light
when he was croaking. I coughed
so hard last night. I was only joking
and the German
had a good idea about plants.
But there were boys when I was a boy.
We took a magnifying glass
and roasted ants. They'd sizzle up.
We were all teeth somehow, boys,
and spit brown juice into cups.
And we all wanted to kill each other.
And in the sun we meant it. Strange.
To want to end our dirty, frayed lives
busy killing ants. We'd cry out
under clotheslines, worrying mothers
to a tread. We were boys, and
their violence, my own violence, my hands,
our greasy hands, light, more light,
in the fireflies burn and press
we buried our dead.

# [The Ticket to Heaven]

Stay & hold me & these suffering
hands. I won't be long.
I will not remain unread like an animal,
for God does come & blows the dust
from my back & says goeth thou into that other
world. Children are here bright as ice-cream parlors,
Through their busy music (I am against this)
their progenitors watch from a torn curtain of light
& they too are good but still here
in Heaven we must worry
because no one ever knows what's coming
not even here where I have come
to sing for the sullen angels. I will destroy the ice trapping
their once furious wings. I came & went among men &
    women.
I saw strange and furious things,
& now like a child I must go
& like a man be silent
& like a woman receive the ghosts
& stand firm like a woman

or a man
& childlike remain tethered
to this good earth where I was at home,
hoping it keeps me here
though I won't be long
hitched here for a second
just a split second, good, so lost & gone.

# [A Victory]

The ocean was black near the shore and farther out a storm was massing in the sky. He sat, looking out over the water, looking up aimlessly at the night from the tiki bar, wondering how it would work out. His arm hurt, and he was ashamed but somewhere inside he was secretly happy he'd beaten his father-in-law at the bar table. The silence between Paul and his wife that night had been as unbearable as the sound of a child that cannot stifle its own cries or be comforted in the middle of the night. It was the silence of a death.

The surf nearly reached the legs of tables and chairs at the beachside bar. The encroaching water sounded against the rocks with hard slaps, lightning broke overhead, thunder followed with a dull, lonesome menace. It was the end of something, the beginning of another path. This was the only way home, if only he'd have seen it. She had left with them hours ago through the rain, heedless of the approaching storm.

"We haven't had a hurricane in long time," the barman said as he wiped the tables and counter of the sticky remains of rum and Cokes and beer. "We never fear them. What will you do, anyway?"

The barman talked on as he slung his dreadlocks over his tawny shoulders, looking out as if he knew what was coming, as if he didn't believe his own insouciance about hurricanes, his eyes lifting toward the horizon as he polished the lacquered countertop.

Paul ordered another beer and sat alone and waited for her to approach him, to admire him again, to forgive. He chatted with the longhaired, garrulous barman, listened to him the way we listen when we are listening so generously that it might save us.

"You beat big man tonight, eh?"
"Yes."
"I couldn't believe how long you both held on. Looked like he break your arm off. But you won," he exclaimed. "You won."

Among a variety of things that had set his wife off was the arm wrestling match he'd drunkenly entered into with her step-father. "Doctor," as if his Christian name had molted after his residency, stood about six feet nine. He was at ease and confident the way professionals often are. He was listened to and heeded quite often, even when he was wrong, because he had a lot of money. His head was a glass-smooth dome with no hint of stubble. He had rescued the family years ago. The biological father had committed suicide years before in a truck with a hose running from the gas to the window. Paul had never met the suicide, but somehow he felt his presence and loved him and when he'd drive past the graveyard back in Flume, MO, he'd tip his hat or say a prayer for him or put flowers on the simple grave. As if his fate was somehow tied to his, Paul hated what had happened to the dead man. He hated that it had occurred, been allowed, perhaps been encouraged.

And his wife Veranda had grown close to her mother in the way a promising flower can be choked out by a competing plant, wasting its fragrance by the side of the road. At first, Paul, in his new role as husband encouraged Veranda to forge a bond or just a relationship with her mother who'd been married herself four times. The mother, a nurse practitioner, forensic in all of her talk, had finally married the doctor to whom she often said abusive, vulgar things when she was drunk or down or happy or up or herself or not. One of her stock phrases always shook Paul.

"Jesus fuckin' Christ, George!" she had screamed poolside a few days earlier after he'd brought the woman the wrong drink. "I asked for Hendrick's!" Suddenly, the good doctor was merely George, a low, biblical name, a simple tag without status.

Even the rich are sometimes at a loss in this world, and Paul could pity them in his way, looking out at the sea from the hillside villa where they'd arranged to stay in Roatan. From where he stood he could see the madness of the blue of the water, the shores of Honduras faint and gray in the far distance. Paul wondered what might happen (as a thought-experiment) if the son of God appeared and served her the requisite gin and tonic. It was only a thought. The rich are too much at home, he thought. They are too comfortable, and this makes them uninteresting. Not even the ocean impresses them, he thought.

When the family left that evening, he stayed back at the villa in order to sneak a cigarette. It had been a long two weeks of furtive drags. Sneaking around like some high school delinquent.

It was after the smoke and looking from the villa in late evening that he'd thought to go down to the bar, down the rock road that lead to the sound of the sea.

The doctor and his wife sat in silence just before the challenge, an offer, a wager that seemed to arise out of spite and boredom. Veranda's mother suggested that Paul and the ready-to-please Doctor compete in order to find out who was stronger, better. "I mean, who's the stud, here?" She'd laughed, tossing around her blond hair.

"No way," Paul answered. "I know I'll lose." He was trying to pacify the table.

"Give it a fuckin' try," his mother-in-law said.

"It's up to him," the doctor muttered.

Veranda sat in silence through the debate around the table. She thought the whole thing stupid and suspected her husband would be humiliated again. Like at the college. Where he'd been dropped as an adjunct and grown so angry and self-doubting that he dropkicked their food onto Lemp Avenue in St. Louis. This was after Veranda had sulked about the bad news at an Italian restaurant. Paul had always expected more of himself, of everyone. But money was money and, in the end, would dictate the terms.

Doctor and Paul joined hands, bracing their elbows against their left hands. He was prepared to lose, to fail again, and did not care so much about the results. He wished he was back in Missouri, alone.

For twenty minutes he thought his arm would snap. The doctor's grip was immense, like a glove of iron clamped around his slender hand. It was as if the doctor, his father-in-law, wanted to hurt him, though the doctor was far too benign to justify this low suspicion. Although competitive, the doctor – and he assumed victory – wanted a good match. His wife looked on with bleary, frustrated eyes, muttering things. (The good doctor, dammit, was supposed to do his job – efficiently). He has started too hard, too soon, Paul thought. I will hold on. I will break my own arm if that's what it takes.

"Get him, George," the doctor's wife screamed, her husband relegated to his Christian name again. Veranda looked sullen and detached from the two men locked hand in hand, as if there was an unspoken love between them. A few stragglers around the beach gathered near the table to watch.

Normally a recluse, Paul fed off of them, because they seemed on the side of youth and on the side of the smaller. The doctor's arms were those of a lifter, much larger than Paul's. The ocean sang in the back, and when the thunder roared, he began to move against the doctor, arcing his hand and trying to redeem all of his defeats, the images of his failures, into one true victory.

When he pinned the doctor — it was over. Veranda's mother muttered something, got up, turned her back on the shabby bar room grapple, and walked away up the hill to the villa. The doctor reluctantly smiled, shook Paul's hand, and followed her a few minutes later into the dark. His eyes were equine from strain, watery from effort.

"I won."

"Yes. You won. It's so stupid."

"I know."

"What's the point?"

"He asked me. Your mother asked me too."

"You should have said no."

"I didn't," he said, the secret, shameful feeling of joy inside him for a second.


Veranda followed her family up the hill along the rocks and later was sleeping while he stayed at the bar. The hurricane was coming on. Palm trees lashed back and forth in the wet winds.


"You did beat him. Was that your… father?"

"No. My wife's father."

"She pretty lady."

"Yeah. Beautiful people can make us do awful things."


The barman wiped the counters and was putting away chairs. Paul thought about the villa and going home and how his arm ached. Perhaps he should have refused. It was, after all, stupid. He rubbed his right bicep with his left hand. The water was being struck by hard rain and he was under the roof of the bar. Hours earlier they'd taken photos by the beach. It had been sunnier then. They had been on their first drinks. They had posed for tourist pictures that a local took. Now the barman sang to himself, some song in Spanish, and he was happy and would walk himself home in an hour to his woman and his child. Paul had little to no idea where home was, how to find his way back, as the storm increased, as it scoured the island. He said a prayer to the Virgin Mary, a prayer to Jesus, and felt absurd. He prayed for himself, for everyone and everything, rubbing his arm. As he walked in the rain toward the villa, he knew he was going back into defeat, that his victory would be swallowed up, forgotten, even by himself. The rain was cool and munificent. The power was out but the lightning flashes gave enough light to find the way back, and Paul could smell orchids and hear palms gnashing.

He waited outside their door, no beacon light in any window. He could hear Veranda, his new, soon-to-be-ex-wife, lightly snoring, and he imagined she was dreaming of a new life. He knew that his arm ached and was bruised. In the darkness he knew the ocean was there, out in the distances beyond the vines, beyond the hillocks of grasses, waiting to receive the waters of heaven.

# [A Small Bestiary Within]

They want a sweet country
boy, tender, true as hell.
At least they seem to—
they do, until failures mark up
his face. Until his tail
even, is short & tucked, & he goes
disgraced as a small-town pervert.
Against the bank.
Against the speculation,
against the theft.
You want to chat
about this? He's the kid there
looking down into the floor.
His own shadow reels inside him.
He paces door to door.
It is restless, his shadow, coiled,
a ready-to-snap snake & he keeps
telling it to calm down.
& he doesn't know exactly
who orders whom.

In the distance a dog howls.
Its bone white rictus grin.
He's closer than ever
to speaking dog.
He's so close.
Let's begin.

# [Adventures in Dentistry]

When my tooth was yanked
out, my mouth turned violent.
The dentist, Dr. J., broke the bank.
I dulled out with Percocet.
The print was blurred on my gazette.
Sipping whiskey through a gauze-strained
gum, I spaced out to cars
swimming just out the door.
Easter would come just after Lent—
Four Roses burned like an open sore.
I thought about cigarettes.
& I was angry & had no rent.
You were angry as I rinsed & spat.
Out of the sewer crawled the rat,
its belly bloated, translucent, smooth.
It shivered & crept down the sewer grate.
Overhead the stars cooed—
they were candles, dying out, reigniting:
I wanted them to flame until our streets were clean.
I wanted the stars – cold enough to eat –
to burn out until there was nothing left.

## [Mother's Day Sonnet]

Little light inside her
that's what you are, a little light,
a terrifying bloom. But I will keep you
tight as a well-made line,
the laundry line stretched through the night
your mother sways beneath.
& my money will blow in gusts,
blue breezes made to hollow
out accounts. & I will be afraid.
I will grieve some for things I've wasted,
for lights I've extinguished, stubbed out
& the lights I've lit up
& seen swarm—my pinwheel, sugarloaf, honey, dear –
land into my arms & squall, summoner.

[As it Is, I]

cry out to the animals. Their souls.
I still hold them, the dead ones.
I keep them in a box that kicks so
hard it's a woman's
belly holding all the secrets.
An old heart. No. My heart
can hear their songs,
echoing a lover's heart that taught me
to wait, to stop & refrain:
the frightened horse isn't beaten
to any good. Praise her
always, for being good & just, still.
I coax her flesh & try
to feel my hands—
sudden birds
along her back.
Simple words for her. I tell her things
about the world & she agrees.
I let her out into the night.

I lead her from the barn
into the winter night. Everything,
everything will be fine. I tell her this
against the frost. Words form
& burst in December. I am close.
I am close to believing these words.
I am learning to let my heart breathe
& take in each true thing.

# [Goodwill]

Evening rustles  round      windows of our     Goodwill
faces   good faces of children – poolfresh – mothers   too
a few confused fathers run  still
run hands   this is guilt free
shopping   frightened     books and pottery
the shards    the shirts   Taylor Swift over  & over
   the satellite
radio     my heart is a busted shoe     radio signals
   my heart
swarms  with blood    marry me    families
their observable silence   here     in a firefly town
we grow tender  as a bruise    last night
I dreamed of you    mother   lover   you— creekfresh
a white dress    your hair disturbed     in breezes
grackle  black   black as the sheriff's new Michelins
you walked somehow   into me   I was good again  going
   nowhere

## [American Standard]

April Fool's  falls on  Easter  this year

 I just thought  you'd like to take that in    here

once  I almost had  a scorpion  for  a pet

its curious tail  struck out  a small flame

from summer's humid porch    long ago winter

had left  but  when those snows—

so many  falling  rooms  silent   on walks    for the cows'

bells  scraping  white fences    O when the snow disappeared—

my father   trapped  the creature    in a mason jar

flushing  the body   its deadly  thorn  far

down into our American Standard

it swam  pointlessly back      to some desert

April Fool's   falls on Easter   it's coming soon

I am alive   &  straddle the world   beneath the moon's

damaged   face  it is a golden coin  I   must  give  back

through America's  economic  plumbing    I will   I will

hurry it     to the hunger stream   I will give   the night

this  gold that vanishes    its worth   stripped   away

peeled back   humiliated      I  celebrate this fool this
   mission.

# [Tonight]

A bit of dust here,
the small sink of dishes flashes.
Slowly agreeing. Anchored
to what was always before us,
I think to order things.
To set the small wrong
into a bit of anonymous good.
To not wear out things
by looking at them too long.
To set the crooked straight.
This happens at holiday parties.
All the eyes drinking in their fair share,
taking in the orphaned furniture,
the glasses no longer brilliant.
You taught me to rest my eyes.
To witness and to see.
How you look so small coming in.
How you are never too worn.
Your morning hum hits the sky's
upper register. I am not damned.

It should have snowed by now,
our eyes renewed from each flake.
That would be something.

# [Sympathy]

Parking meters squeezed me out of glitter towns,
& so, I moved deep into the sticks.
The Baptist Association spreads the Word.
Oaks & cedars along 47 groan & whip
the shadowed backs of our fissured roads.
Even bad Catholics still have sympathy
for the small efforts of our rock n roll,
fire & brimstone brothers & sisters,
hands raised in valediction,
their children sent to deserts, hard missionary work.

I get out onto the shoulder,
& beneath a white tent,
a pastor who's recently called his son
douchebag in a restaurant,
preaches the world's plummet
& the Word's ascent.
I miss my woman, I suppose.
Her ease, her body, the afternoon
drowning out my own ideas,

the pastor's orations little birds,
grackles that float toward the blue,
& in their wake, it's suddenly Spring.
I get it. I do. We want our spiritual cake,
& we want to devour it too.
Turn your face from all that light.
Wipe your mouth. Look into the eyes
of each sacred body that has failed,
stumbled, risen up & cried out.
When I see billboards about the unborn child,
I worry. On the drive home, I can hear a squall
climbing, creeper vine filling up the skull.
A life projected & thrown
off into the world. I go on,
worried, listening to my bank balance
frittered on a speaker phone.
Douchebag, I think. That's all I am,
& the future is coming,
roiling & real & unstoppable.

# [Champagne]

I was in love with the black stripper in the ways you'd
    think.
My friends fed me Adderall and fuel, as we howled,
crashing into a populated skating rink.
Her name was Champagne, her thong was pink.
It broke my heart when, on a starless winter night,
I kissed her stomach just above the brink
of her sweet warmth.  You're workin' harder than me,
    mister,
she sang into my lovesick ear. Come morning,
the club lights still spun as I hunted
her, but mostly looked for Ramen and juice.
I could hear the auctioneer's voice from his midnight
    booth.
In the local Walmart she'd hold
her little boy's hand through the islands of debris.
It was all ache to see her arrowed eyes
scan a coupon and hope everything was free, whispering
love back into her boy's ear.
I had kissed the spot that bore him and,

as we roared a one-way street
my friends, my grateful, jealous friends and I—
we waited for the light.  I had known the boy's earthly source.
The work was worth it when I was ultimately harmed.
On the way out through the windshield, I reached out for his arm.

# [Christina]

There's a good woman visiting
me tonight well-known for her grace & hair.
These are my cigarettes.
There is anticipation & beer.
But we frown on so many gifts.
We truly do. Once, I saw horses'
breath against December air.
It's like that. This waiting.

## [To Be of Use]

I sit at the banks of the Missouri
as evening hums with mosquitoes.
My breath is bourbon warm.
In winter you'd see it spark the air,
gunmetal dust the color of bone.
You'd know it was me until we crawled
against the rivers of sheets.  You'd know I waited.
A pool of sweat ribbons from your ribs.
You tell me each day is the first day of summer.
You fall asleep and don't startle
when the violin string snaps.
I have come here to love and to be loved.
That was all.
The music and drinks were lovely, unnecessary
accessories that warmed our throats, hearts.
It's neither warm nor cold.
I crawl into bed and imagine falling through sheets,
a warm impress of work mornings left quickly.
I want to be loved.  I want to be of use.

# [Here Again]

Only say the word
& I shall be
here, right here
a black bird
shivers
buries itself into the red
maple leaves
the day grows gray
settling down
onto my road
I can somehow hear
the river
the river
it is too near
& you are gone today
I am happy here
not having the right
words, but these only—
& only say the word.
I will come forth.

[How We Grew Thirsty]


I can't help it. I smile when our teapot cries and steams.
Or when the dogwoods ignite along our street.
I can't help myself. I grin. I dream, demanding more than the dream
& its sudden death at nine.
And isn't your face – so part of mine pressed to the windowpane?
Why do we hike up our jeans now, shoes full of ash?
All of the things that drew us to light your quick hands now strangle out the rain.
As if earth & air had throats. As if, after spring, its two-faced attack of flood & swollen fjord, you'd choke out the last spirit of the god.
Help me see what it is you see along this aimless, barren road.
Help me take on your terror.
I will clothe myself in this grief,
its end-of-days rattle & turn.
I will zip myself up in flames.
I will see you better when we burn.

## [Simple Song]

The lamp blooms and we turn old.
Credit scores go down a perpendicular chart.
Children slide on gray sheets of ice.
Money can't buy happiness, love.
The crickets sing that it might be nice.

# [Sneer]

With each oyster-like gob that comes de profundis,
with phlegm that coats the side of my hatchback,
I feel disdain, but for life now.
I sneer and smoke like a poolhall bitch.
I sneered too when I was asked to snitch on boys
who beat off in bathroom stalls.
You could hear them, their final squalls.
They rested their heads on desks in math.
It was after lunch, then home where there was a cold
bath waiting for their backs to receive strokes
of leather belts. I think of them.
I smoke and think of Aaron, his right arm
vacuumed off in a combine. He was reported
not to have cried out but fetched his ruined limb.
The boy carried it back to the farmhouse. How he'd smoke

    in stalls.

How the crows that day must have spread like India
ink, their caws from tree to tree.
How different everything must have been.
Standing on the corner of this and that.

I wear a Stetson and pull down on my hat and wait for a
 stranger to pass by.
I still get paranoid when I get high. I touch both arms
with both hands. Like some ruined, rained-on puzzle,
there are pieces missing. I walk, light up,
and think of boys running through the gym, high as kites,
singing something about rubber and glue, their high-tops
 squealing
above this impossible brightness.

# [We're All Hunting Something]

My candy red car
has swerved & negotiated
from the bars,
with ditches & with the grass.
It's made of horny flames
kissing down the black
tires & the windows down,
as our hair was speed hungry
to its ends, thirsty,
our strands blackened out factory
flames. And I want the car back.
Now. In this July garage and wash.
Jim Bowland waddles out,
five-week beard & flannel rags,
singing in the heat. The sun
raises our hands to our temples.
He's reset the computer in the car.
It's all Greek to me, but I love it here,
with each dent & scratch
pulled, polished, for each dead bug

& anxious bird & these doubts
to vanish. For the wheels to purr
until they will one day rust right out.
I am in a sense betting on this ride.
It comes steaming out of the carwash
as a few girls shy off & a boy shuffles
after them & just as he's gone, he's
left me with the keys again.

## [The Piano]

The sudden ear, electric and astonished:
somber, I am told, rhymes with you, hombre.
I think of a shadow, l'ombre. The shadow
that rules my life. All unmarried
bachelors run merrily from their wives.
Quel dommage! I lost my summer millionaire
by December's dark gray road. My sudden ear
green and bent. Hombre, words lift: where's
the money that I spent? And always here.
Just be, here: words riot the summers up
the air. A million bees now gone, honeybear.
Thank you, master hombre. Penumbrae scatter
into the mouth of the breath of the clutched heart
of the Christ breathing out the world. Bless you, skeptic.
Thank you, O voice, notes, over the sound of these
    heavy keys

Raphael Maurice is a poet, translator, and teacher. He resides in Washington, MO where the river keeps its secrets.

www.ingramcontent.com/pod-product-compliance
Lightning Source LLC
Chambersburg PA
CBHW030140100526
44592CB00011B/983